Vol 9

MAZE

Ages 4-6

FOR KIDS

MAZE BOOK

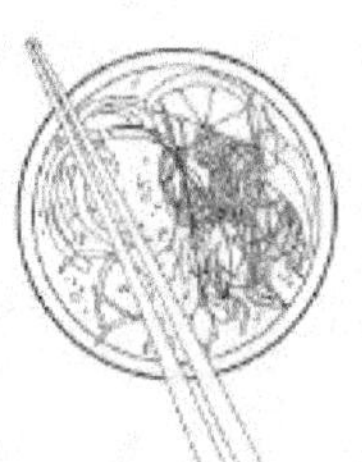

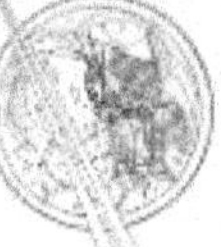

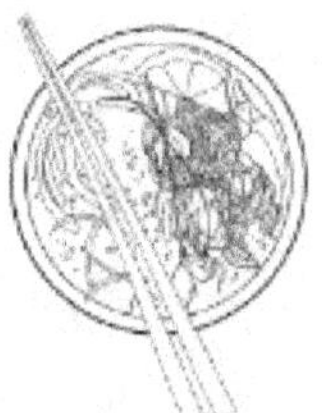

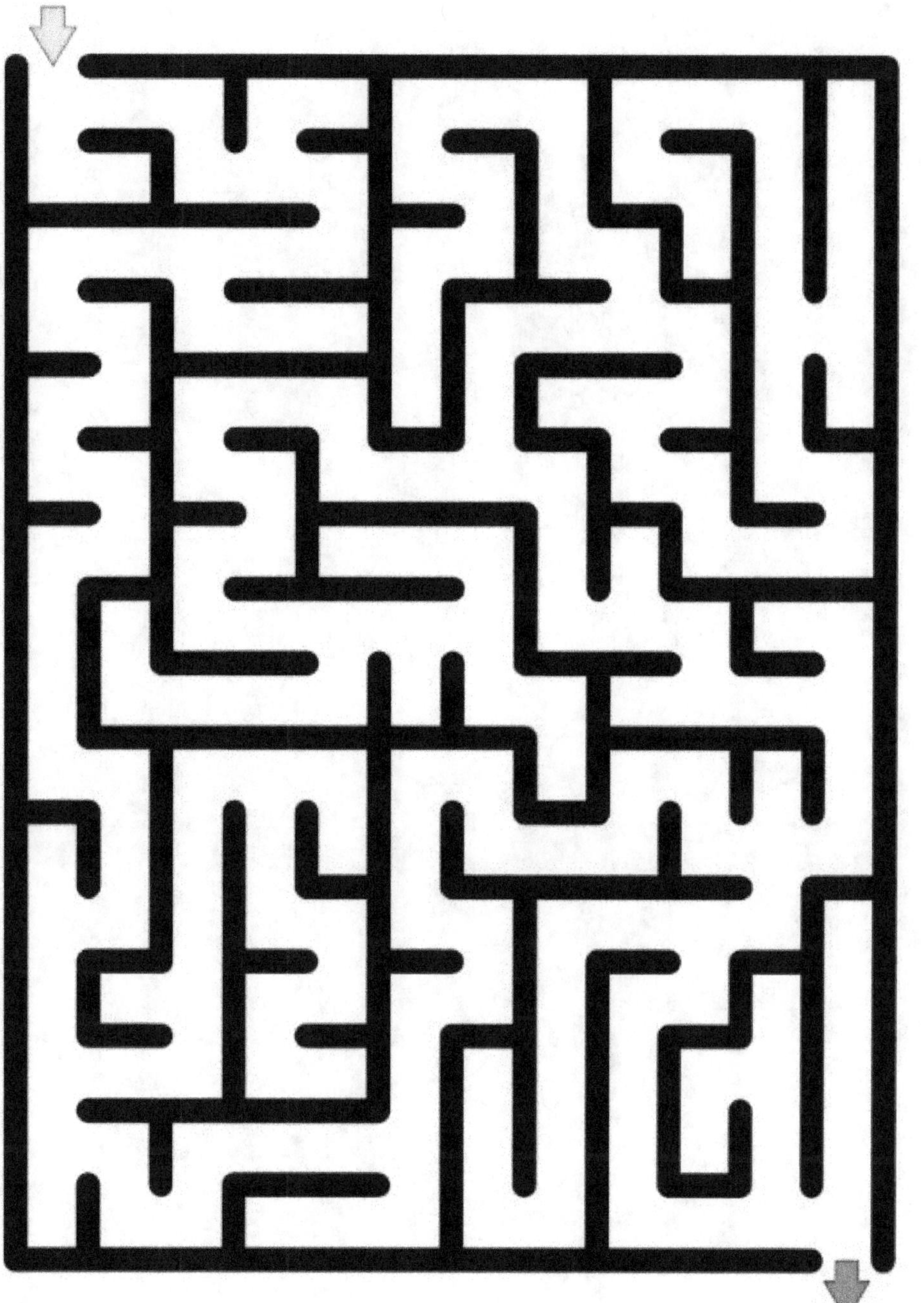

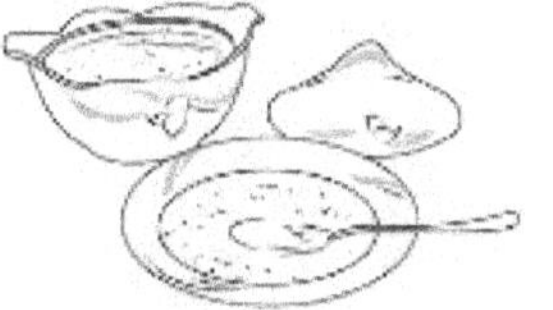

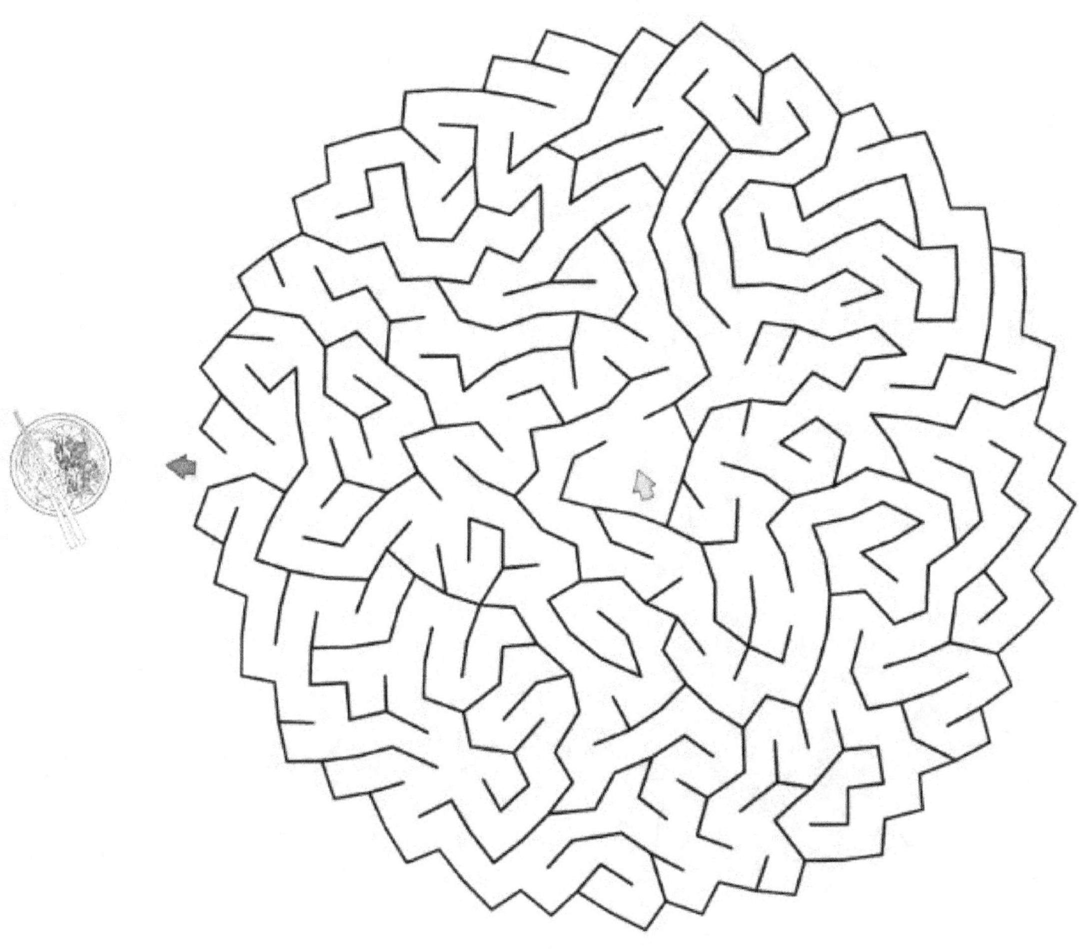

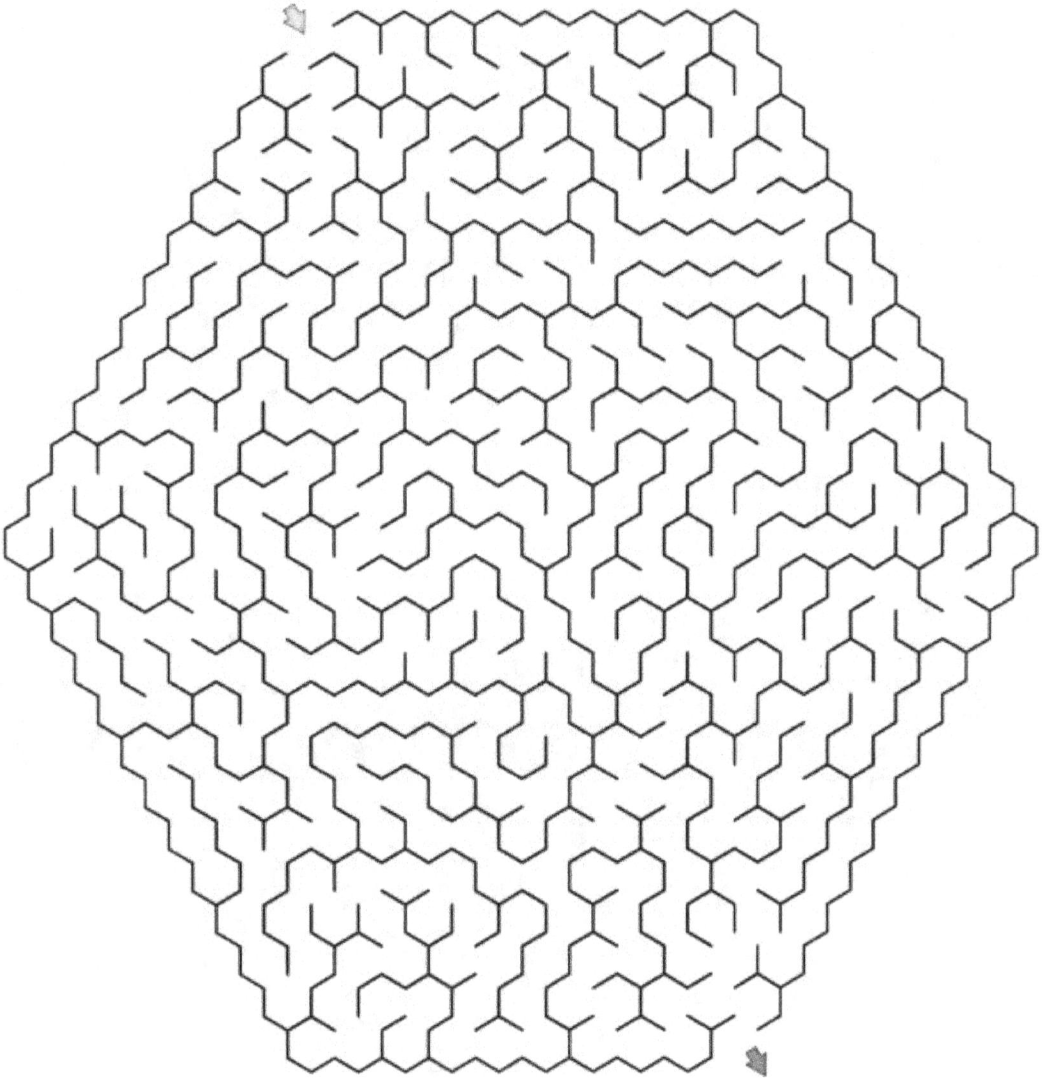

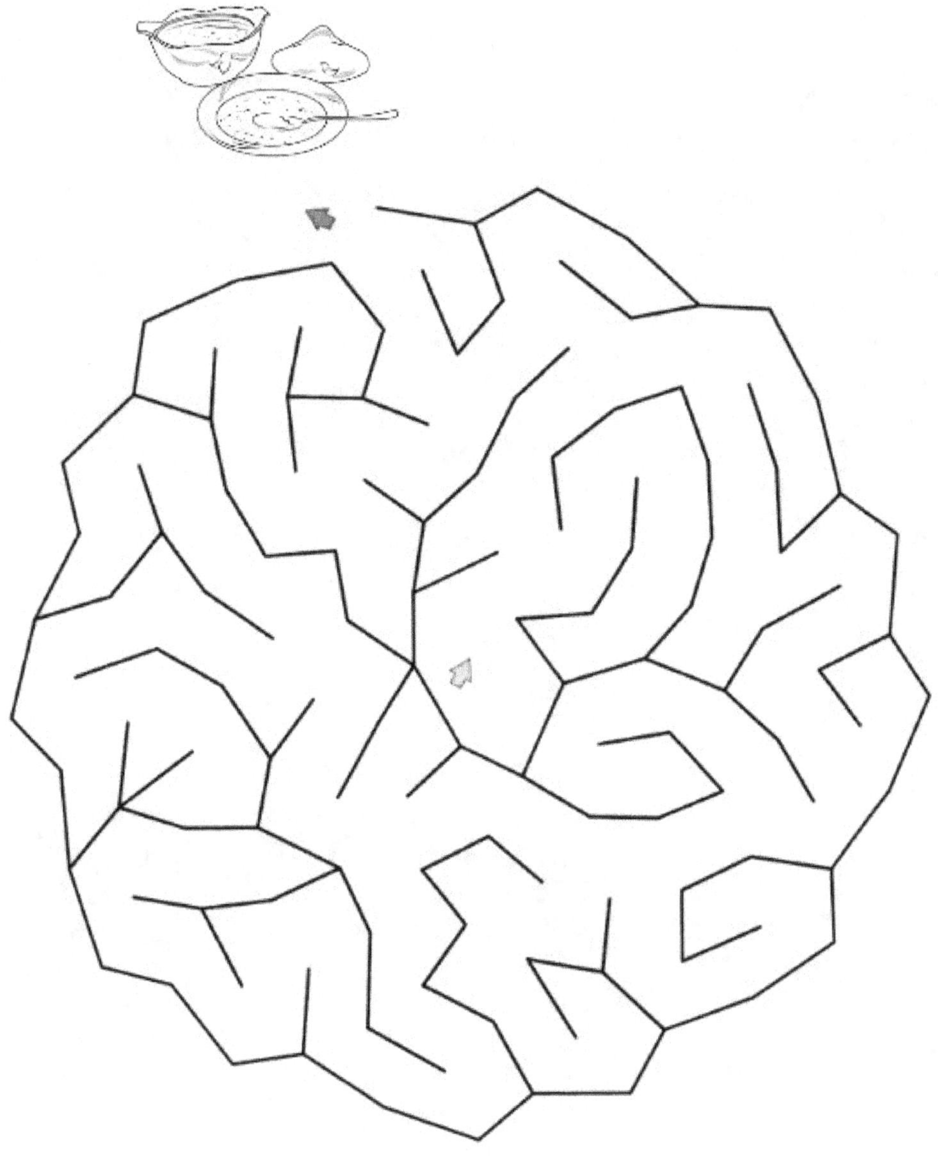

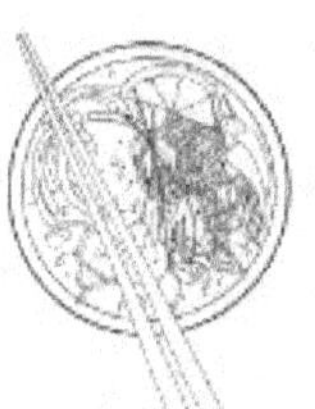

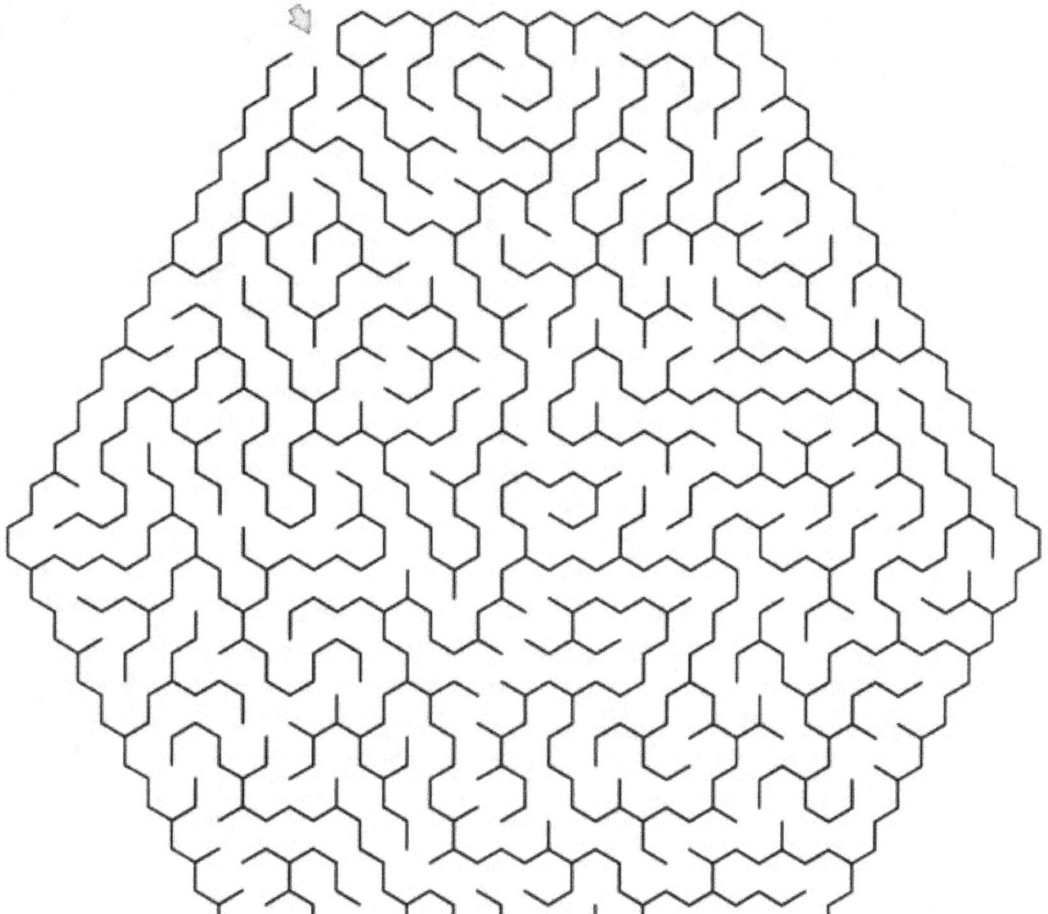

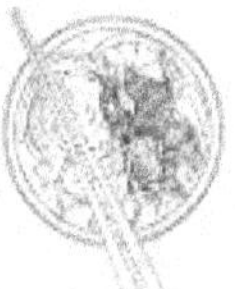

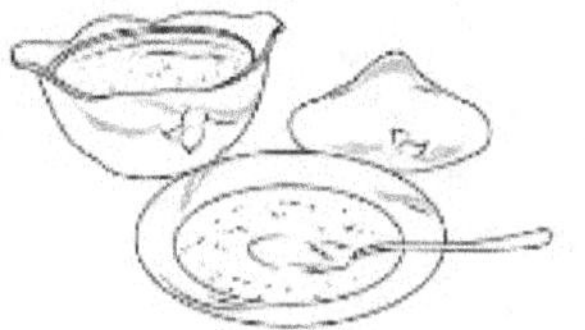

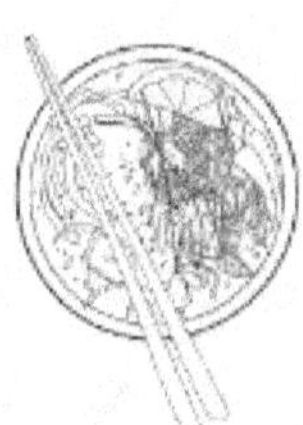

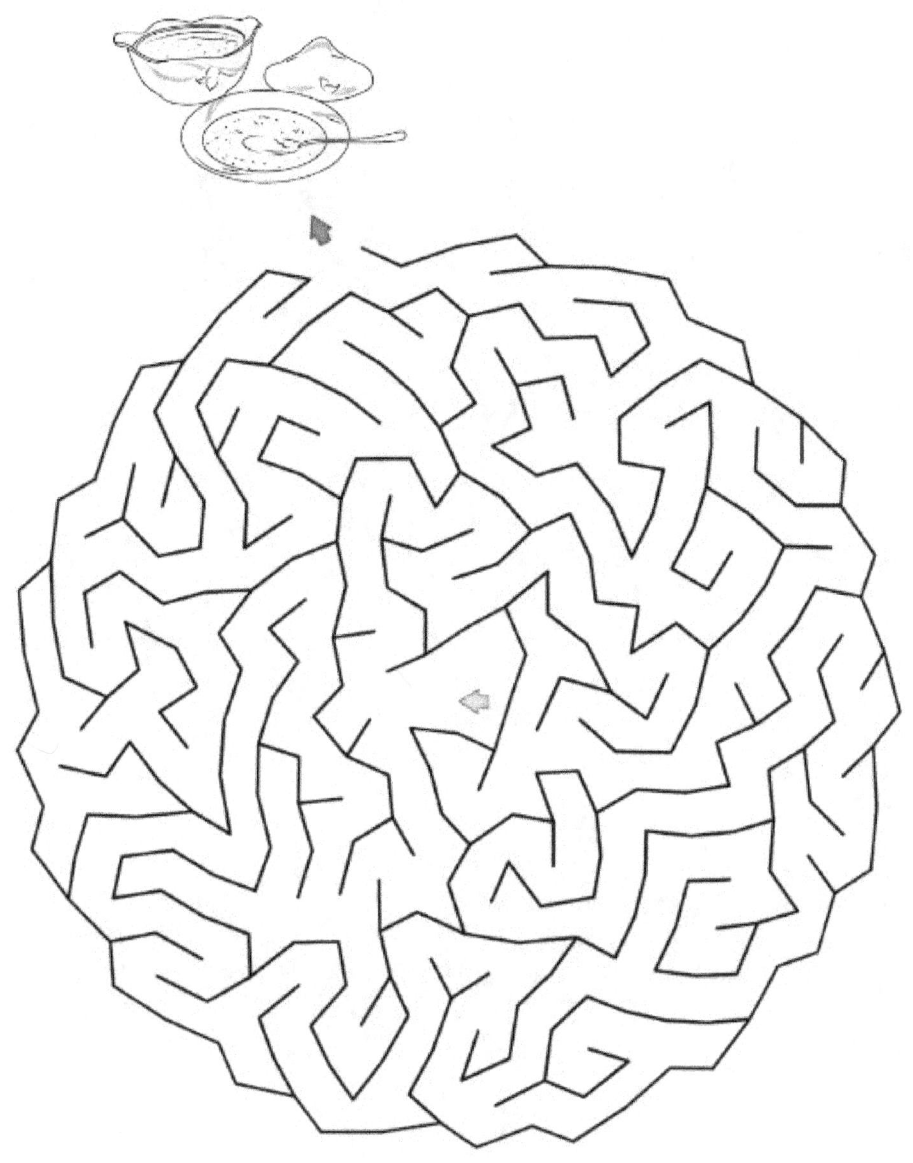

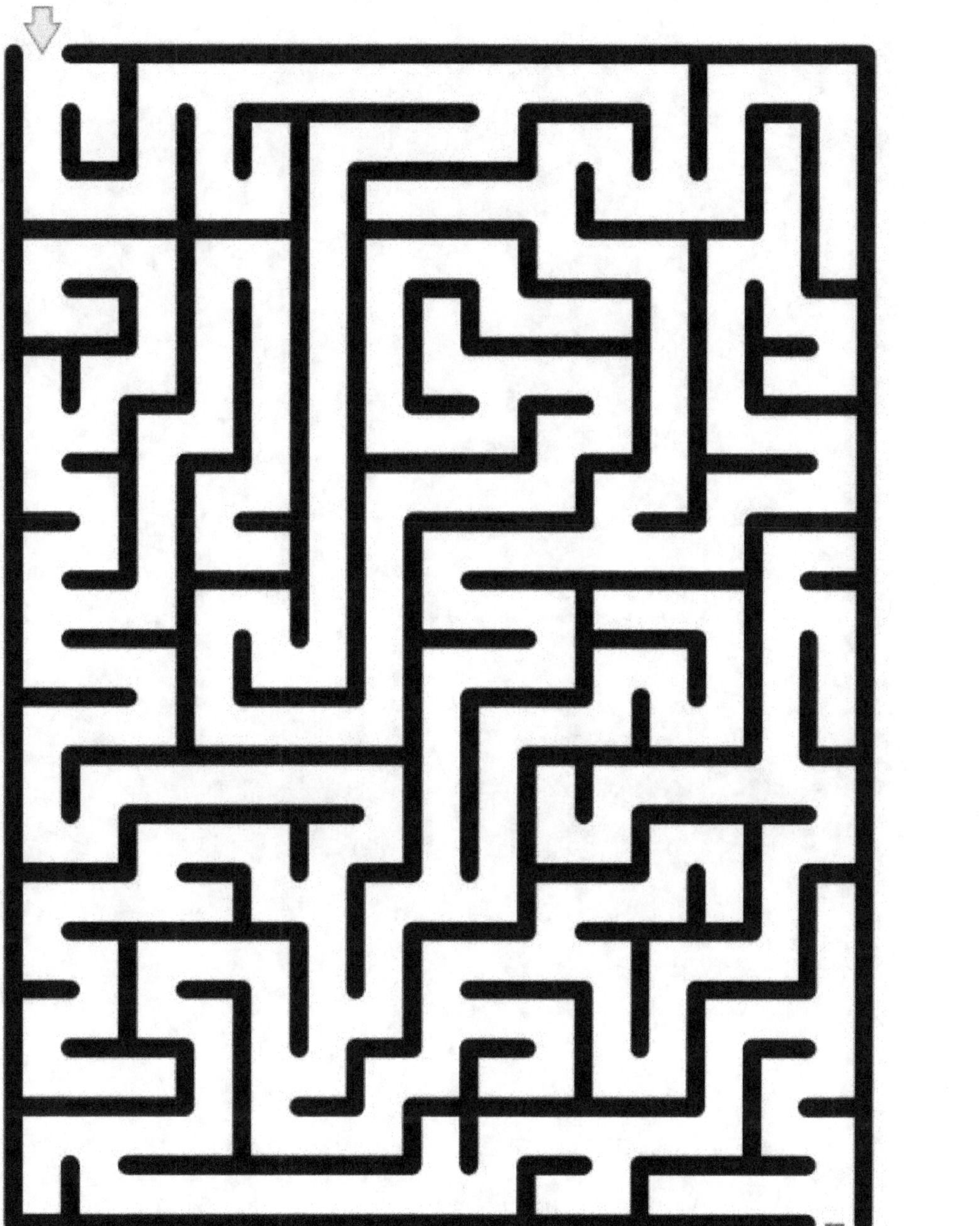

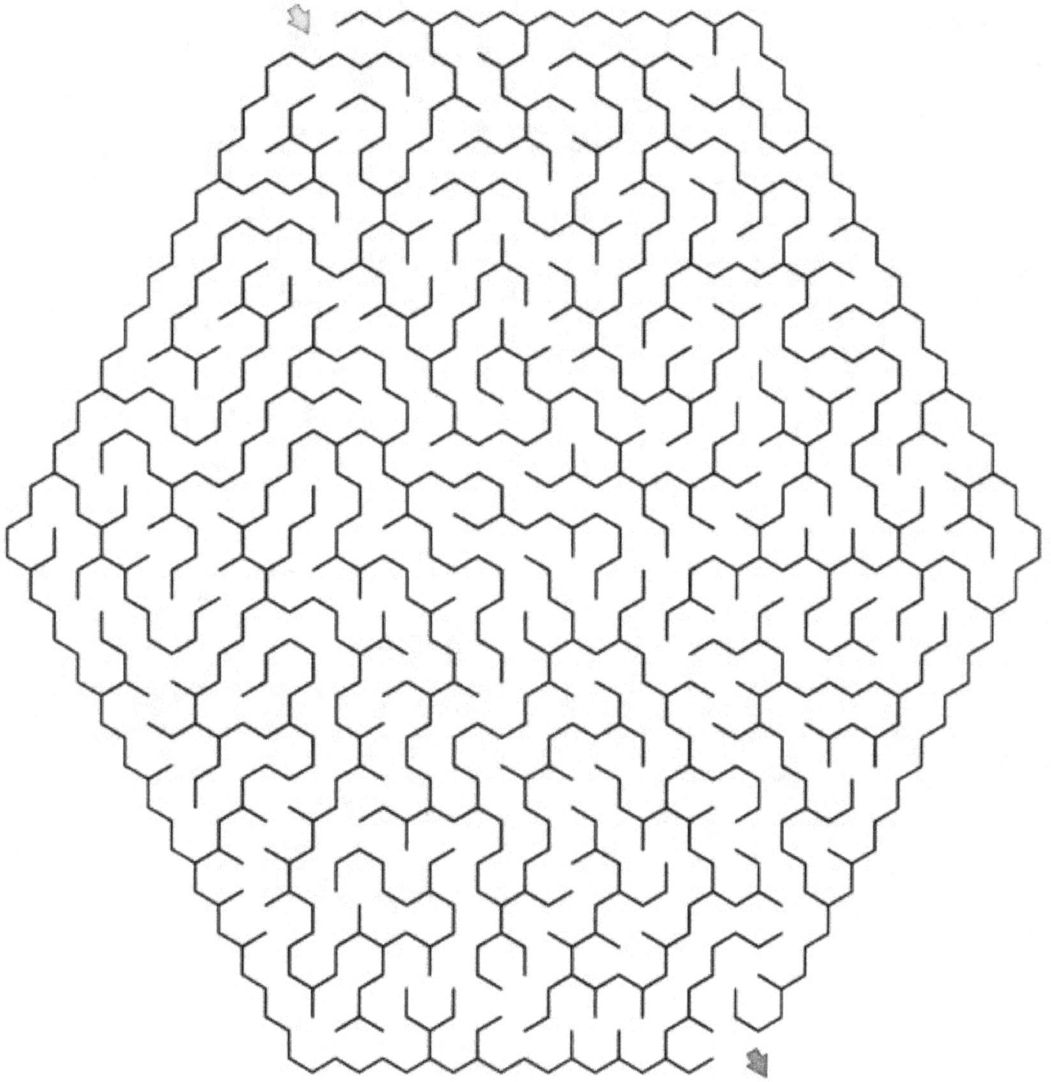

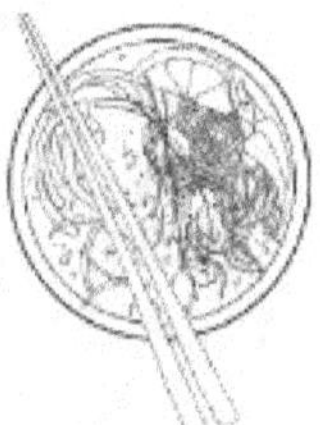

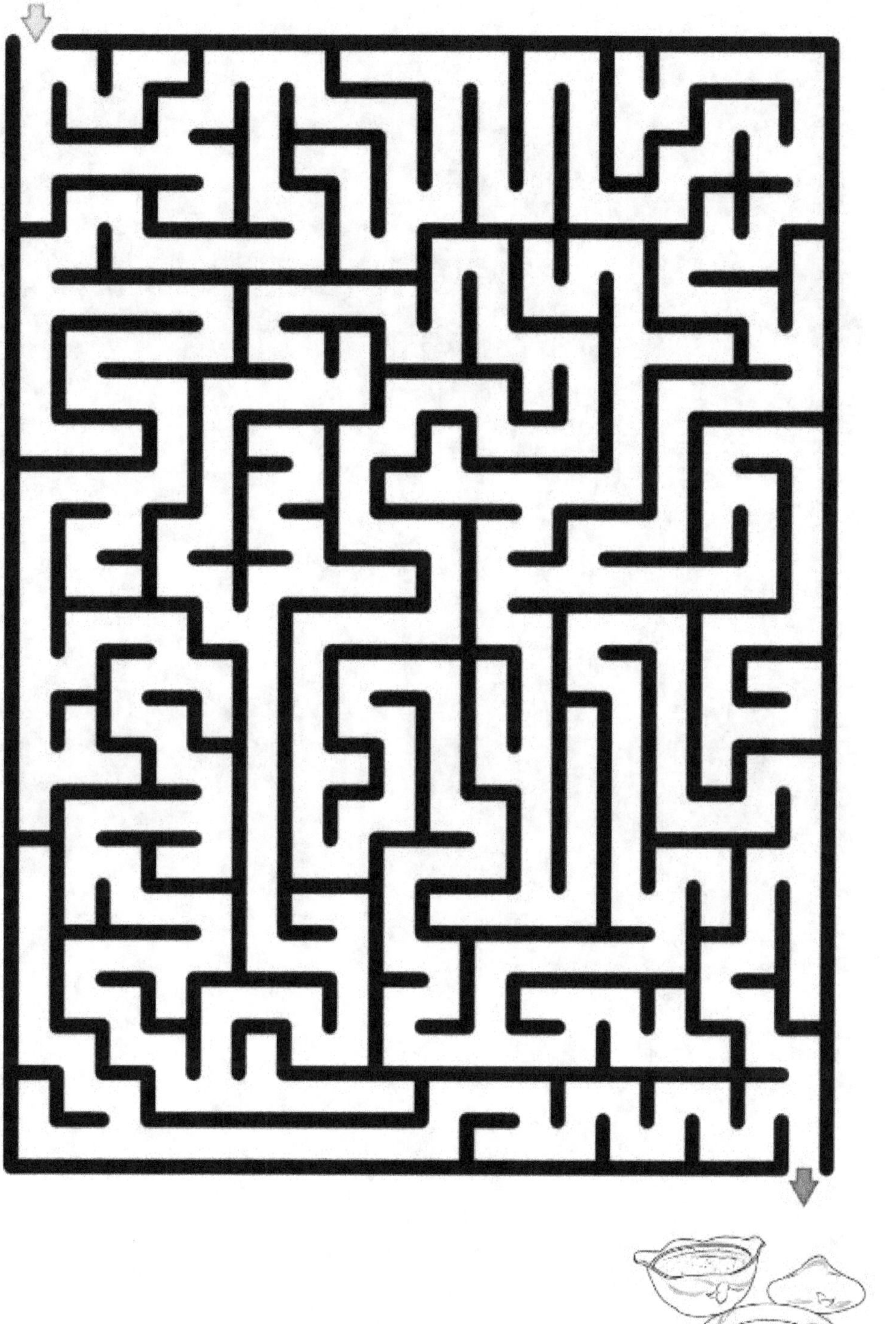

www.ingramcontent.com/pod-product-compliance
Lightning Source LLC
Chambersburg PA
CBHW081737250726
48657CB00010B/3311